America's Forests

America's Forests

written and photographed by
Frank Staub

A Carolrhoda Earth Watch Book

Carolrhoda Books, Inc./Minneapolis

For Debbie

Carolrhoda Books, Inc., c/o The Lerner Publishing Group
241 First Avenue North, Minneapolis, MN 55401 U.S.A.

Website address: www.lernerbooks.com

LIBRARY OF CONGRESS CATALOGING-IN-PUBLICATION DATA

Staub, Frank J.
    America's forests / written and photographed by Frank Staub.
      p.   cm.
    "A Carolrhoda earth watch book."
    Includes index.
    Summary: Examines the growth and changing nature of forests,
the plants and animals living there, and the uses to which these
lands are put.
    ISBN 1-57505-265-2 (alk. paper)
    1. Forest ecology—Juvenile literature. 2. Forests and forestry—
Juvenile literature. [1. Forests and forestry. 2. Forest ecology.
3. Ecology.] I. Title.
QH541.5.F6S735   1999
577.3'0973—dc21   98–7291

Manufactured in the United States of America
1 2 3 4 5 6 – JR – 04 03 02 01 00 99

CONTENTS

Spring sunshine filters through the new leaves of a forest in the Smoky Mountains of North Carolina.

Imagine a squirrel running through the treetops from the Atlantic Ocean to the Mississippi River without ever touching the ground. That might have been possible when white settlers first arrived in North America. In those days, much of the eastern half of the continent was one continuous forest.

The forests were a familiar sight to those early white settlers. Similar oaks, maples, and pines grew in the forests of their European homelands.

But as other settlers made their way west in the 1800s, they encountered forests like they had never seen before. The vast stands of pine, spruce, and fir blanketing the Rocky Mountains were quite different from the eastern forests. The settlers could hardly believe their eyes when they first saw the towering redwoods and the enormous giant sequoias in California. No other trees on earth are taller than the redwoods or bigger than the sequoias.

Although many of those trees were cut down over the years for lumber or to clear the land for farming and building, some still survive. Throughout the continent, forests continue to thrive, and they remain one of America's largest and most varied natural environments.

Near the California coast, a grove of redwoods reaches for the sky.

TREES AND MORE

A place where trees grow—that's how most people think of a forest. But a forest is much more. It is made up of many other kinds of plants as well. And dwelling among the plants are a variety of animals. Still, trees are the biggest forest plants. They provide food and shelter for the living things around them. Many of a forest's plants and animals would quickly die without trees.

A stream flows through a New Hampshire forest, which is made up of different kinds and sizes of trees.

Like other plants, trees have roots, stems, and leaves. Roots anchor plants in the soil. Stems, or trunks, hold up branches. And branches are covered with leaves.

It's the roots' job to take in water and nutrients from the soil. Nutrients—including phosphorus, potassium, magnesium, calcium, and nitrogen—are the substances that plants need to grow and stay healthy. Soil nutrients come from organic matter—pieces of plants, dead animals, animal waste, and anything else that has come from living things. Soil with lots of organic matter is rich and fertile and holds water well. Sandy or rocky soil has few nutrients, so it is poor and infertile. Water tends to drain away through sandy or rocky soil quickly, leaving little for plant roots to absorb.

Roots absorb water and nutrients, which move up through the trunk to the branches and leaves.

The smooth bark of a birch tree peels off in papery layers.

Trees have a single stem, or trunk, rising up from the roots. The trunk and branches are covered with bark, which protects the tree from wind and snow and hungry animals. The outer layer of the bark is no longer alive. Pieces of it fall away in patches. The bark of different kinds of trees falls off in different ways. That's why the bark of each kind of tree looks unique.

Beneath the bark is the wood. Nutrients and water move up thin tubes from the roots, through the wood in the core of the trunk, to the branches and leaves. The wood layer is hard. Trees can grow tall without flopping over because wood makes their trunks stiff. Bushes or shrubs contain wood, too. But unlike trees, shrubs have many woody stems rising directly from the roots. A shrub's stems are so thin that if they grow too tall, they bend over and break. That's why most shrubs don't grow taller than you or me.

Leaves are a plant's food factories. They trap the energy from sunlight with a chemical called **chlorophyll.** Chlorophyll is what makes leaves green. The trapped energy is combined with water and a gas from the air called carbon dioxide to make sugars. The sugar-making process is called **photosynthesis.**

Sugars are a plant's food. They are used for energy. They are also used to make many of the other needed chemicals in a plant's body. Sugars flow down from the leaves to the rest of the plant through the live, inner layer of bark.

In climates with cold winters, photosynthesis occurs only during the warmer months. This important period is called the growing season. It is the only time plants grow and produce seeds.

Chlorophyll makes leaves green and helps the tree make food from sunlight.

Forests are like tall buildings with many floors, one above the other. But instead of floors of concrete and steel, forests have levels formed by trees, shrubs, herbs, and soil. The arrangement of a forest's different levels is called **stratification.**

The highest level in a forest is the **canopy**, where the trees' top branches join to form a leafy ceiling. In some forests, the canopy may be 200 feet (60m) above the ground. The next level is the **understory,** made up of younger trees and smaller trees, such as flowering dogwoods and vine maples, whose tops are beneath the canopy.

Below the understory is the **shrub** layer of bushy plants with many woody stems. Beneath the shrub layer is the **herb** layer of soft-stemmed plants—ferns, grasses, and wildflowers. Unlike trees and shrubs, herbs have no wood in their stems so they can't grow much taller than a few feet. The soft stems and branches of herbs die each winter, and new stems and leaves grow back each spring.

Some understory trees, like the vine maples at the bottom of this picture, live only in the understory and will never become part of the canopy. Other understory trees will grow and eventually become part of the canopy.

In an old-growth forest, fallen trees covered with moss cause bumps on the forest floor.

A layer of fallen branches, trees, and leaves called **litter** covers the forest floor. Beneath the litter, the soil itself forms the lowest forest level.

Forests with young trees, old trees, fallen trees, and **snags**, or dead trees that still stand, are called old-growth forests. Almost any forest can be called old growth if it's been around long enough. But the words "old growth" most often refer to forests that have never been cut down.

NEEDLES AND LEAVES

America's forests contain two main kinds of trees—**conifers** and **broadleaf** trees. Conifer seeds come from cones, and their wood is usually soft. Most conifers, such as pines, spruces, firs, and hemlocks, have thin, needle-shaped leaves. Two other kinds of conifers, cedars and junipers—have leaves that look like rows of little scales. Most conifers keep their needles or scales all year round. They are **evergreens.**

Broadleaf trees, including oaks, maples, hickories, birches, and poplars, have wide, flat leaves. Their seeds come from flowers, and their wood is often hard, so many broadleaf trees are also called hardwoods. In places with freezing winters, the leaves of broadleaf trees fall off during the autumn and grow back in the spring. Plants that lose their leaves for the winter are **deciduous.**

Douglas fir cones hang from branches covered with short, round needles (top). Red cedar leaves look like rows of scales (middle), and gambel oak leaves are rounded and flat (bottom).

14

Deciduous tree leaves turn color in the autumn and fall off by the time winter comes.

When the temperatures drop and the days shorten as winter approaches, photosynthesis in deciduous trees stops. Then the chlorophyll breaks down. Without the green chlorophyll, red and yellow chemicals in the leaves show through, and the yearly fall color show in deciduous forests begins. Without chlorophyll, the leaves can no longer make sugars, so they have no further use to the plant. Soon they die and fall to the ground.

Most conifers hold onto their needles all year long, even through cold, snowy winters.

Plants lose a lot of water as it **evaporates** from their leaf surfaces. Water evaporates by changing from a liquid into a gas. When the ground freezes during the winter, the roots can't absorb any water to replace what evaporates. To hold on to the water they already have, deciduous trees have another reason to drop their leaves.

Conifers don't lose as much water through evaporation, because their needles are smaller than most broad leaves and they have a thick waxy coating that holds water in. The needles also contain a chemical that keeps them from freezing easily. That's why most conifers don't need to lose their needles during the winter.

In general, conifers can live in more extreme climate conditions than broadleaf trees. If the soil is dry and infertile, or if the winters are long and cold, or if the winds are fierce, a forest will usually contain more conifers than broadleaf trees.

FORESTS FROM SEA TO SEA

From the Atlantic Ocean to the Pacific Ocean, nearly every U.S. state and every Canadian province has some kind of forest, however small. Different regions have different forest types because of differences in local weather and soil. Only certain kinds, or species, of trees are found in each forest region.

The Forests of North America

Boreal Forests
Transition Forests
Eastern Deciduous Forests
Southeastern Forests
Subtropical Forests
Woodlands
Montane Forests
Subalpine Forests
Northwestern Forests

It's too cold for trees to grow in the Arctic lands near the North Pole. But farther south, where the summers are warmer, vast conifer forests of black spruce, balsam fir, and white pine cover much of Alaska and northern Canada. A smaller number of hardy broadleaf trees—including quaking aspen and paper birch—share the region. This is the northern or boreal forest region. Snow covers the boreal forest floor during most of the year. When the snow melts, the ground gets so wet that a boreal forest is sometimes called taiga, a Russian word meaning "swamp forest."

In a damp, frosty boreal forest, the spring and summer growing season lasts a mere three to four months—not much time for a plant to put out new leaves, make sugars, grow, and reproduce. But because they keep their needles through the winter, the conifers are able to start making sugars as soon as the growing season begins.

Since conifer needles stay on the tree all year, they block the life-giving sun of spring and summer from shorter trees and plants. With so little light beneath the canopy, few plants can grow. As a result, boreal forests dominated by conifers are not well stratified. The herb, shrub, and understory levels are poorly developed.

A boreal forest in Alaska is dominated by conifers. Beyond the lake lie the snow-covered Wrangell Mountains.

South of the boreal region, in southeastern Canada and northern New England, New York, Michigan, Wisconsin, and Minnesota, summers are a little warmer and the growing season lasts a bit longer. These milder conditions allow more broadleaf trees—including sugar maples and yellow birch—to thrive. Conifers found in the boreal forests live here, too, along with others such as eastern hemlock and red pine. With large numbers of both conifers and hardwoods, this is an area of change or transition between the northern conifers and the broadleaf forests farther south. This in-between land is called the transition forest region.

Transition forests aren't as dark as boreal forests because the canopy opens up when the deciduous trees don't have their leaves. More plants can grow beneath the canopy trees. These plants include young trees, berry bushes, and springtime carpets of flowering herbs—violets, wood lilies, and trilliums, among others.

Wildflowers, such as bloodroot, grow on the forest floor in transition forests.

In an eastern deciduous forest in Pennsylvania, most of the trees have lost their leaves for the winter.

South of the transition forests, winters can still be cold, but the growing season lasts half the year. During the growing season, there's plenty of rain. Here hardwood trees greatly outnumber the conifers. This is the eastern deciduous forest region. Like transition forests, most eastern deciduous forests are well stratified, with many herbs, shrubs, and understory trees.

Each spring, before the leaves grow in and block the sun, light streams down between the bare branches to the deciduous forest floor. The forest plants come alive with new leaves and flowers. The plants grow and reach for the light quickly, before the canopy leaves grow in and cast their summer shade. When autumn comes and the canopy leaves fall, it's too cold for the lower plants to do any more growing. They wait through the winter, until the spring sunlight returns.

Leaves on deciduous trees in the Ozark Mountains of Arkansas begin to come out in early spring.

The kinds of trees vary in different parts of the eastern deciduous region, depending on climate and soil. Beeches and sugar maples dominate many forests in Connecticut, Pennsylvania, and other states in the Northeast, where winters can be cold but the soil is usually rich. Since sugar maples grow well in shade, they often populate the understory.

Soils are generally less fertile in parts of Missouri and Arkansas, but the winters are milder. Here, oaks and hickories litter the forest floor with acorns and hickory nuts. Enough light reaches the forest floor for blueberry, huckleberry, and laurel bushes to thrive.

The southern Appalachian Mountains in Virginia, North Carolina, South Carolina, and Tennessee contain North America's greatest variety of tree species in their sheltered ravines. Azaleas and rhododendron fill the shrub layer with flowers every spring. Tulip trees tower over the redbud and flowering dogwood in the understory.

Dogwood blooms grace a southern Appalachian forest in the spring.

In many parts of southern New Jersey, the soil is too dry and sandy with too few nutrients to nurture most hardwoods. But pitch pines, Virginia pines, and some oaks can grow in the sandy south New Jersey soils. The pines give the area its name—the New Jersey Pine Barrens.

South of the eastern deciduous forests, in the southeastern forest region, there's a good amount of rain and the growing season lasts most of the year. But the soil is often sandy and dry. So the most plentiful trees are pines—shortleaf, longleaf, loblolly, and slash pines. The southeast has some hardwoods too, however, such as oaks, hickories, hawthorns, and hollies.

New growth covers the forest floor after a fire in the New Jersey Pine Barrens.

The Florida strangler fig looks like a tree, but it's actually a vine. It roots into a tree branch and eventually strangles and kills the tree it is growing on.

The southeastern forests extend into Florida. But in southern Florida the weather is like that of the tropics, with plenty of moisture and a year-round growing season. In addition to pines, coconut palms and 100-foot-tall (30m) Florida royal palms grow in the subtropical forests of southern Florida. The hardwood trees are the same as those found in the hot, humid jungles of Latin America and the Caribbean—including West Indies mahogany and gumbo-limbo. Unlike the deciduous hardwoods farther north, most subtropical hardwoods are evergreens. They keep their leaves all year like most conifers do because southern Florida winters aren't much colder than the summers.

A piñon pine grows in the foothills of the Rocky Mountains in western Colorado.

West of the Mississippi River, much of North America is too dry for trees to survive. Grasses cover most of the Midwest's plains, and deserts occupy much of the Southwest. Those forests that are in the West are usually dominated by conifers.

Most western forests are in the mountains, where there's more rain and snow than in the lowlands. In the lower slopes, or foothills, of the Rocky Mountains, just enough rain falls for trees to grow. With so little rain, trees don't always grow close enough together to form true forests. Instead, they form **woodlands,** where the branches of neighboring trees usually don't touch. Woodlands are more sunny and open than forests, with grasses and wildflowers growing among the trees. From Idaho to Mexico, "pygmy" woodlands of short piñon pines and junipers cover much of the lower foothills.

A little higher in the foothills of the Rocky Mountains, there's just enough rain and snow for larger pines like the ponderosa, the most plentiful tree in the United States. The word "ponderosa" refers to the tree's ponderous, or massive, size. A ponderosa pine's long roots take in the large amounts of water these big trees need.

Children hike through a grove of ponderosa pines in the upper foothills of Colorado.

Quaking aspen turn golden in the autumn. Most of their branches are near the top because their leaves need lots of light.

Above the foothills, the air is cooler, with more rain and snow. Here we find the true forests of the mountains—the montane forests. In the Rocky Mountains, some montane forests have a mix of ponderosa pines and Douglas firs. Others are made up entirely of densely growing lodgepole pines or groves of quaking aspens. When the aspens' leaves quake in the wind, the whole forest shimmers.

Above the montane forests, the winters are long and cold and the growing season is very short. This is the land of the subalpine forests. A subalpine forest is a lot like another land where winter rules—the boreal forests of the far north. Like a boreal forest, a subalpine forest is dark and poorly stratified, with few understory trees, shrubs, and herbs. High in the cold, snowy Rocky Mountains, Engelmann spruces and subalpine firs grow.

Englemann spruces and subalpine firs tower over a hiker in a subalpine old growth forest in the Rocky Mountains.

Winters are milder in California's Sierra Nevada, so oaks grow well in the foothills. Oaks can't take the cold as well as many conifers can. But, like most pines, many oaks can grow in poor, dry soil.

The montane forests in the Sierra Nevada and the mountains of southern Oregon are also called mixed conifer forests. Over twenty different kinds of conifers live here—more than anywhere else in the world. They include ponderosa pines, sugar pines, Jeffrey pines, red firs, white firs, incense cedars, and giant sequoias. Giant sequoias are the world's largest living things. At the base, some are as wide as a small house.

The General Sherman tree, a giant sequoia in California's Sierra Nevada, is the world's largest living thing.

High in the Sierra Nevada subalpine forests, Great Basin bristlecone pine, foxtail pine, and western juniper grow out in the open. Many trees are gnarled with wind and age. Low-growing shrubs spread over the ground or in crevices between rocks.

The northwestern forest region is the realm of America's grandest forests. It stretches along the Pacific Coast from northern California to Alaska. Winters here are short and not too cold. Summers are often dry, but winds blowing from the Pacific Ocean bring steady rains and thick fog during most of the year. These ideal growing conditions for conifers make the Northwest home to the world's tallest cone-bearing trees. The redwood is the world's tallest living thing. This relative of the giant sequoia can tower over 350 feet (100m) into the air.

A highway called the Avenue of the Giants cuts through a grove of redwoods, the world's tallest trees.

Farther north, in the northwestern old-growth forests of Oregon, Washington, and British Columbia, conifers such as western hemlocks, western red cedars, Douglas firs, and Sitka spruces reach incredible sizes. Unfortunately, less than ten percent of our original northwestern old-growth forests still stand.

Hikers wear rain ponchos in a wet, mossy, old-growth forest in Washington State.

It takes nearly 200 years for a northwestern forest to be considered "old-growth." Most are 350 to 750 years old. Some are over 1,000.

Sunlight is limited in the northwestern forests where conifers grow close together. As a result, many northwestern forests have few plants growing beneath the big trees. But when a tree falls, a space opens for light to stream down and support a lush growth of herbs, shrubs, and understory trees.

CREEPERS, CRAWLERS, CLIMBERS, AND FLYERS

The different levels of a forest allow a variety of animals to live in the same spot, one above the other. Birds fly through the canopy, squirrels and porcupines crawl on the branches, deer nibble on shrubs, and slugs inch along on the forest floor. Like the floors in an apartment building, each forest level has its own residents. Each animal has its own niche. An animal's niche is what it does, what it eats, and where it lives. A niche is like an animal's job, diet, and address rolled into one. Older forests and forests that are highly stratified offer more niches than younger or poorly stratified forests.

In many ways, forest animals have it good. They have lots of food and places to hide. The trees and other plants block the cold winds of winter and offer cool shade on hot days. But for fast-flying birds, trees and branches can get in the way. Small birds with short wings are best suited to forest life. Large birds like eagles, vultures, and hawks land on branches at the forest's edge or canopy top, but they rarely risk flying the obstacle course between the branches.

Forests provide places for animals to find food, hide from enemies, raise families, or simply rest. A bald eagle (top) perches high on a branch, and a white-tailed deer (bottom) nibbles on a branch near the forest floor.

34

With all the trees and forest plants, it can be dark and hard to see in a forest. The dark-furred fisher is one mammal that takes advantage of the forest's darkness. Without being seen, it can sneak up on porcupines and other animals it eats. Other animals stand out. Male songbirds want to be seen when it's time to attract mates and scare away other males, so they are often brightly colored.

In a dark forest, sound can be just as important as sight. Birds call and sing from the treetops to get each other's attention. Foxes have good hearing to hear the mice, squirrels, and other small animals they hunt. These little animals have good ears, too, so they can hear foxes and other enemies like owls. But owls are very quiet flyers, and they often catch small animals unaware.

The dark fur of a fisher (left) *makes it harder to spot in a dark forest, while a red fox* (right) *has big ears to hear what it can't see.*

Most amphibians, such as the northwestern salamander (above) and the Pacific tree frog (right), can't live in very cold climates.

Where the winters are cold, animals need a warm coat of fur or feathers. But it doesn't get very cold in the southeastern, subtropical, and northwestern forests. So animals without warm coverings—such as snakes, lizards, turtles, frogs, and salamanders—are more common in these milder forest regions than they are farther north or high in the mountains.

BREAKDOWN AND RENEWAL

Some of the smallest forest life-forms are the most important, for they make nutrients available to plants. Insects and worms nibble on the litter on the forest floor, breaking it down into smaller and smaller pieces. Bacteria and fungi then feed on the little pieces of leaves, twigs, and dead trees. Bacteria—microscopic, one-celled life-forms—feed on animal wastes as well as on the bodies of dead animals.

As bacteria and fungi dine, they release the nutrients in their food back into the soil. This process of breaking down organic matter and returning nutrients to the soil is called **decomposition.** If it weren't for decomposers like insects, worms, bacteria, and fungi, the soil nutrients would get all used up and none would be available for new plants to absorb.

A banana slug crawls on a mushroom in an Oregon forest.

This huge mushroom grows in Oregon. Note the boots.

In forests, the most common fungi are mushrooms. What we think of as a mushroom is really just the flower-like part of the fungus. The rest of the fungus is a web of long, thin threads running through the soil or inside a rotting tree. The threads are usually too small to see.

Some fungi help plant roots absorb nutrients. Fungal threads encircle a plant's roots and take in nutrients from the soil. Then the plant roots absorb some of the nutrients from the fungi. In return, the fungi get food from the roots. Certain trees living in poor soil can't survive without their fungus partners.

A dead tree is a good place to see decomposition at work. After a tree dies, beetles, termites, worms, and other tiny animals dig holes into the wood. Then fungi move into the holes. This may start to happen while the tree is still a snag. Fungi soften snags and fallen trees, allowing other plants to take root in the rotting, nutrient-rich wood. In this way, the dead tree becomes a nurse log for new plants.

A rotting tree on the floor of a transition forest provides nutrients for lichens and fungi.

THE CHANGING FOREST

Forests change constantly, sometimes suddenly. In 1980, when the Mount St. Helens volcano erupted, thousands of acres of big trees were flattened by the blast. Windstorms and avalanches sometimes cut paths through a forest. But forests usually grow back after such calamities. New trees and other plants have grown over the volcanic ash that spewed out of Mount St. Helens. And sun-loving species such as aspen and lodgepole pine appear in the space opened up by an avalanche or windstorm.

When Mount St. Helens erupted, thousands of acres of surrounding forest were blown down. In the first decade since, a new forest has begun to grow.

Spruce, fir, and other conifers can grow in the shade of quaking aspen, but aspen can't grow in the shade of the conifers.

Some changes to a forest are more long lasting. Sand dunes, pushed along by the wind, sometimes bury forests. And when water backs up behind a beaver dam, trees die as their roots drown.

Other changes in the forest take many years to occur. For example, quaking aspens need lots of light. They can't grow in the shade of a conifer canopy. But some young conifers can grow in the shade. After 70 to 100 years, those conifers can grow above the aspens. The tall conifers create year-round shade beneath them. Starved for light, the aspens die. In this way, a conifer forest gradually replaces an aspen forest.

The change from one type of forest, such as an aspen forest, to another, such as a Douglas fir forest, is called **plant succession.** The Douglas fir forest is the climax, or final, community. The aspen forest is the subclimax community. Trees of a climax forest can grow in the shade of a subclimax forest, but once the climax forest has taken over, the subclimax trees cannot survive.

41

One of the most dramatic ways a forest changes is by fire. Lightning and careless people are the main causes of forest fires. Fires may be dangerous, but they are part of the natural cycle of life in many forests. Surface fires, which burn only the litter, herbs, and shrubs on the forest floor, do little harm to the big trees. As surface fires burn piles of dry forest litter, they keep them from building up into larger piles. If there is enough litter on the forest floor, however, a fire's flames could reach the canopy, killing the trees. When flames spread through a canopy and burn an entire section of forest, it's called a crown fire. To reduce the danger of crown fires, foresters often set small, controlled surface fires. This gets rid of dangerous dry litter buildups.

In Yellowstone National Park, a crown fire killed the trees in this forest (left), but the ash it left behind fed the herbs that sprang up after the fire (right).

Thick bark protects trees from a surface fire fueled by the litter on a forest floor in Georgia.

Fire also helps increase soil fertility by turning the litter on the forest floor into ash. Plant roots absorb nutrients in the ash right away, more quickly than through the slow process of decomposition.

Surface fires can sweep through southeastern pine forests every two or three years. The thick bark of the adult pines only gets singed, while the dry litter and smaller plants turn to ash. Some of those small plants might be young broadleaf trees, which could grow up and shade out the pines. Broadleaf trees are the climax plants throughout most of the Southeast. But frequent fires, along with sandy soil, keep them from taking over. In the West, fire keeps understory trees from taking over forests of ponderosa pine, giant sequoias, and lodgepole pine.

Fires are rare in some types of forests. Boreal forests, transition forests, eastern deciduous forests, subtropical forests, and northwestern forests don't burn often, partly because they are so moist.

LANDS OF MANY USES

Forests are more than simply trees—they are interrelated communities of trees, shrubs, herbs, fungi, bacteria, and all sorts of animals. Some of America's forests are owned privately, and some are owned by the states. In addition, the National Forest Service manages 156 national forests, owned by all Americans. The National Forest Service's motto is "Land of Many Uses." That's because our national forests are used in many different ways. They are important sources of water, minerals, and food for animals. People take to the woods for everything from mountain biking to skiing to bird watching to hunting.

National forests are also America's main source of the timber used for making paper and for the lumber used in buildings and furniture. The cheapest and easiest way to harvest timber is by clear-cutting. In a clear-cut, the entire forest—trees, shrubs, herbs, and animals—is removed. New trees are usually planted in a clear-cut. But what develops is more like a tree farm than a forest. It contains just one tree species and exists only to produce timber. It soon falls to the chain saws and bulldozers, too. It never grows into a rich, old forest like the one it replaced. Creatures who depend on the big trees, snags, fallen logs, and various plants of a mature forest never return. And without them, a forest is not a forest. It's just a place where trees grow.

In the foreground, the forest has been clear-cut. An old-growth forest still stands at left, and a second-growth forest is growing in at right.

GLOSSARY

broadleaf: a type of tree that has broad, flat leaves. Most broadleaf trees are deciduous.

canopy: the crown, or highest level in the forest, where the trees' top branches join to form a leafy ceiling

chlorophyll: the green chemical in plants that uses light to change water and carbon dioxide into plant food

conifer: cone-bearing tree. Most cone bearers are evergreen, and most have thin needle-shaped leaves or sharp rows of scales.

deciduous: plants whose leaves change color and fall off when the temperature drops in autumn, and grow new leaves when the temperature warms up in spring

decomposition: to rot or break down into smaller parts

evaporate: to change from a liquid to a gas

evergreen: a plant that stays green year-round rather than dropping all its leaves in one season. Most evergreens are conifers.

herb: a soft plant that has no woody stems and whose green foliage dies all the way down to the ground each autumn

litter: the layer of decaying organic matter on the forest floor

photosynthesis: a plant's way of using sunlight to make plant food and oxygen out of water and carbon dioxide

plant succession: one type of forest taking the place of another

shrub: bushy plant with many woody stems that grow near the ground

snag: dead tree that stands in a forest

stratification: the levels of a forest, formed by trees, shrubs, herbs, and soil

understory: the level of forest just beneath the canopy, made up of trees that are slightly younger and smaller

woodland: stand of trees thinner than a forest, with sparse enough rainfall that branches of neighboring trees don't usually touch

INDEX

ABOUT THE AUTHOR

Frank Staub is the author of several books for children, including *Yellowstone's Cycle of Fire*, *America's Prairies*, and *America's Wetlands*. He has also written dozens of magazine articles and created numerous film strips and slide sets. Staub holds degrees in biology and zoology. He works as a freelance writer and photographer, which allows him to travel and study the places and events that interest him most. When he's not working, he climbs mountains and enjoys sea kayaking, bicycling, and sky diving.